DNA OF A CUCKOLD - WIFE EDITION

The Key To An Amazing Marriage

ALLORA SINCLAIR

DNA Of A Cuckold - Wife Edition

©2021 by Allora Sinclair

All rights reserved. No part of this publication may be reproduced, distributed, or transmitted in any form or by any means, including photocopying, recording, or other electronic or mechanical methods, without the prior written permission of the publisher, except in the case of brief quotations embodied in critical reviews and certain other noncommercial uses permitted by copyright law. For permission requests, write to the author, addressed "Attention: Permissions Request," at cuckoopublishing@gmail.com

The publisher and the author make no guarantees concerning the level of success you may experience by following the advice and stratagies contained in this book, and you accept the risk that results will differ for each individual. The testimonials and examples provided in this book show exceptional results, which may not apply to the average reader, and are not intended to represent or guarantee that you will achieve the same or similar results. It is meant as a source of valuable information for the reader, however it is not meant as a substitue for direct expert assistance. If such level of assistance is required, the services of a competent professional should be sought.

Front Cover Illustration by: Stylepics

To Shawna and Lexi. Both you ladies have helped me understand my self and my husband outside the expectations of society. I would have completely missed the mark without your guidance and love.

Chapter One
WHY THIS BOOK

Hi. My name is Allora and I'm an alcoholic. Na, just kidding, but I hope I've put a smile on your face to make you appreciate I do not intend this book to beat around the bush. Chances are, you have this book in your hands because your husband has nervously asked you to read it? If not, then I'm going to suggest you skip this chapter and move on to the next.

For all the women left, welcome.

If you have looked at the cover of this book, you're probably asking what the hell is this book about and why did my husband give it to me? Is it some kind of erotic novel? A step-by-step sex position Kama Sutra kind of thingy? Let me put you at ease. This is neither. It's a book to introduce you to the world of cuckolding.

Okay, what is cuckolding? We'll get into that in the next chapter but, before we do, you must understand the how and the why this book is in your hands.

Your husband wants to either introduce you to or clarify what is going on in his mind. This takes guts. He has probably wanted to tell you for a long time. To him, he feels like you are going to judge him, think less of him or even worse, make you want to leave him. Trust me when I say, you do not fully appreciate how lucky you are yet. Your husband loves you and desires you more than you could imagine.

So why has he essentially asked some random woman named Allora to design a book for his wife? Well, for starters, I am a cuckoldress. Yes, that means my husband is a cuckold (cuck for short). We have been married for nine years and have had a cuckold dynamic for over seven of those years. I have been down the path your husband is hoping you, too, will want to take. So, I'm going to have a solid understanding of what your thinking and feeling as we explore this little thing called cuckolding.

You should also know that there is a good chance your husband has already read, watched or listened to a ton of information on the subject before he has gotten to this point of sharing this with you. He wants you to read this book because he is ready to come clean and disclose what is going on in his mind and his heart.

Your knee jerk reaction to all this is to become fearful, concerned or frustrated. He can't tell you straight? Why not? He may have already mentioned cuckolding to you. Perhaps his attempt was an epic fail, or perhaps the way he told you was disturbing, or perhaps even disgusting in your mind.

I intend to set things straight so you, at the very least, understand your husband. Perhaps cuckolding is not for you, and that's okay. But, you need to realize, to your husband, it is a driving force to who he actually is. He did not choose this, just like you did not choose to be the daughter of your parents.

As you go through this book, you're going to learn some things about your husband that most would consider embarrassing and shameful. Remember, there is nothing that he has done wrong, it's the way he thinks. Likewise, you may come to discover some things about yourself that you did not realize were there. Discoveries you probably would not want to admit to yourself, let alone your closest of friends.

I want to provide you with a roadmap or a blueprint that offers a gentle, clear and undistorted view of what cuckolding is really about. If you crack open your smartphone or laptop, you'll find a myriad of highly eroticized renditions of cuckolding that in reality is the farthest thing from the way it really is.

Take comfort in knowing your husband wants you to read this because he wants the absolute best for you. Nothing else. If it's not your cup of tea, then you move on. Also, know that this is a very difficult discussion to navigate without feelings being hurt or egos getting bruised. Hence this book exists to help smooth the discussion along.

Finally, I realize you are now asking yourself, "Okay, this is all great, but get to the point. What the hell is cuckolding all about?" That's next. But, before we go there, I want you to realize the potential gift your husband has given you. Being a cuckoldress is like being at the very top of the food chain. Having the world revolving around you may not be your thing, but please keep an open mind. Your husband disclosing that he is a cuckold is possibly the best thing that could happen to most women.

Chapter Two
SO WHAT EXACTLY IS CUCKOLDING

The term "cuckolding" is historically rooted in the behaviors of the cuckoo bird secretly laying its eggs in other birds' nests. I know right. What?! The history of how and where the term came from never excited me either, so let's just skip to the chase.

In the modern-day, cuckolding is a relationship dynamic within a committed relationship (usually a married couple) whereby the husband is a devoted, kind, loving and monogamous partner. The catch? The woman (or wife usually) is free and encouraged to go outside the committed relationship to engage in sexual relations with others.

Simple, right? Not at all.

To put the icing on the cake, in a cuckold relationship, the cuckoldress (wife) is enabled power and control over the relationship beyond the bedroom. She wears the pants, no questions asked.

The cherry on top? She typically will have complete

control over the household finances, does little to none of the household chores AND...as this kind of relationship develops, the cuckold (husband) begins to live in a life of complete ecstasy and bliss, knowing all the above, approving of it and in fact, encouraging it.

So, now you're thinking to yourself 'WTF!?!? I get to have sex with any guy and my hubby willingly allows it, doesn't rage with jealousy, and does my laundry while I spend his money to get some sexy outfit for the next guy?'

Yup. It makes little sense, but here's what you need to know. If your husband is a cuckold, and I suspect he is if he has asked you to read this book, he knows this makes no sense. That's why he has probably struggled to say anything about it at all. He is painfully aware of how messed up this kind of thinking is. Believe me, if you asked him, he wishes this kind of life did not feel so right inside of him. It makes his life a potential misery and makes you consider the possibility of leaving him.

On the surface, cuckolding seems like a crude, distorted and somewhat perverted way to want to run any marriage. It takes the concept of fairness and makes fun of it. It twists the idea of loyalty to where you're not even sure if loyalty at any level could exist. And then it holistically makes love look like it's just going to evaporate if this lifestyle was to exist.

Wrong, wrong, wrong.

Here's a fun fact. Multiple studies that have conclusively proven that cuckolding in many instances can improve the quality of marriage significantly for both partners. It seems counterintuitive, but many things in life work that way. Poor example here, but take chemotherapy.

It is a highly directed poison to kill cancer cells. It also kills some good cells (hence why most people become violently ill during therapy) but also ends up saving your life. Taking poison that feels like it's going to kill you but saves your life. Again, I know, a terrible example, but it makes the point.

The key to cuckolding is that it works ONLY if you are both on the same page and that your baseline relationship health is already good. It will in no way save a weak marriage. It will probably destroy it or, in a best-case, damage it significantly. Make sure you are solid as a couple before you consider this direction.

Your husband has likely gone on an intellectual journey of self-exploration before coming to you. This is huge for him to expose this little side of himself to you and know that you could rebuke or think less of him. Before you say anything to him, I would ask that you reserve questions or judgement until you have read the next couple of chapters. One will help you understand why your husband is the way he is and the second will look at helping you self examine to see if cuckolding is something you may also find is a closer fit to who you really are.

Cuckolding is a very multi-layered lifestyle and personality type. It is not for everyone. For many, it's not just something that does not appeal to them, it's also something they cannot engage in. Most men would be in horror if their woman was to have sex with another man. Again, I'd like to repeat, your husband did not choose to be this way. Cuckolds have a masochistic side that runs through their DNA, just like you have blue eyes or green. No decision to have a certain eye color is ever made. It just is.

Finally, I want to caution you to not explore the

internet on this topic...at least not until you finish this book. This lifestyle is arguably the most extreme of alternative lifestyles, making it grossly misunderstood by much of society and completely misrepresented in most of the porn world. Let's examine things in real terms that are not scary or distorted.

Chapter Three
IS THERE SOMETHING WRONG WITH ME?

The first question you will probably have when you are told what cuckolding is, why? Why does my husband want me to have sex with other men and get nothing in return? The first logical answer you will come up with is, 'he must want to cheat on me or he already has cheated and feels guilty for it'? Nope. Then you'll likely question his sexual interest in you. 'Do I not do it for him anymore? Is he gay'? Again, nope. Then, once the reality of what cuckolding has sunk in, you're likely to question if or how your husband could love you if he wants you to have sex with other guys. I mean, who does that?

Speaking from my own experiences when davie (my husband) dropped the bomb on me, I was a hot mess. I thought this was the end of what I thought was our very happy marriage. Little did I realize that it was the beginning of a marriage that is better than I ever thought possible.

It's important to understand that there is nothing wrong with you or the way you're thinking and feeling. It is normal and natural. This is scary, and let's face it, a bizarre thing to be told your husband is not only okay with but would also prefer to see happen.

Please understand, this has nothing to do with you at all.

Warning, another terrible example coming.

Let's pretend you're a young adult and you've been dating this man for a couple of years now. Every time you want to get intimate, he pulls away and makes some excuse. Finally, he discloses that he is actually gay and only finds other guys sexually attractive. Is that your fault? Did you cause him to be gay? Can you do anything to change him to find you sexually attractive? We both know the answer is no on all counts. He was born that way.

A similar thing is going on with your husband. He does not want to have a marriage that is less than perfect. Cuckolding is, by design, a marriage mixer upper in a very large way. In the initial stages, it can put enormous strain on your relationship, cause feelings of anxiety, fear and doubt and can drill holes to the very foundation of the marriage, making things very unstable. Believe me, he does not want to be this way. Chances are, he has been fighting this need for several years and you are now finding out because he can no longer live a life that is misaligned with who is and who he deeply wants to be.

A rather large misconception many of my girlfriends make is wrapping their heads around how their husband could allow them to have sex with another man and not be raging with jealousy. To a non-cuck, this would be the reaction. To a cuckold, they feel that jealousy, probably more than you could imagine. The thing is, this emotion is filtered through their little cucky brains differently than most. As unpleasant as this feeling is, it turns them on. In fact, the more jealous they feel, the more aroused they get. I know it makes no sense, especially if you are a cuckoldress. You would likely be a lunatic if your lucky husband was to have sex with another woman. That's why this type of relationship only works if you are both on the same page in polar opposite directions. Believe me, his failure mostly to show jealousy is not a representation of how much he loves and cares for you.

The silver lining in all this is, cuckolds worship their wives, even if they never actually embark on the cuckold journey as a couple. You have done nothing wrong. It is entirely rooted in your husband's deep-seated needs at a genetic and primal level. The real question that you should ask yourself is are you from the same 'DNA' family? I use this terminology loosely. The literal context would make you blood relatives and, well, that's just sick. What I mean is, are you a cuckoldress? Like your husband, do you possess the same distinct attributes that make cuckolding so successful and rich for most couples that travel down this path?

Before you try to answer that, you need to understand that this kind of relationship will only work with one type of couple. You can both walk the path of swinging or hotwifing (I'll explain them in the next chapter if you don't know) but cuckolding is unlike both kinds of alternative lifestyle sexual adventures. Cuckolding is like opening a pandora's box. You become immersed in a sort of all-consuming way. To the true cuckold and cuckoldress, it allows them both to reach a physical, mental and emotional plateau that is achieved no other way. The way I felt was like finally being released from a long-term jail sentence. I felt so free and empowered; it was euphoric. Davie intensified the feelings of being right by my side as my cheerleader. I could do no wrong, be as selfish as I wanted and with every move, davie would greet me with a smile and a deep passionate kiss.

Chapter Four
THERE'S MORE ?

Now you're asking yourself, 'What could possibly define me as a cuckoldress and what the hell is the difference between that and a hotwife or being in a swinging relationship'? All excellent questions. Let's start by clarifying the difference between these three.

A swinging relationship is when both the husband and wife knowingly and mutually consent in sexual relations with people outside the marriage. Typically, they will do this together in the same room. Sometimes, they may venture out on their own, with the other person fully aware of what they are up to. It enables both people to explore their sexual appetite with other people without the element of cheating or infidelity becoming a factor. This kind of sexual dynamic can add some serious spice to marriage and is probably the most common form of non-monogamy relationship out there. It is NOT for everyone and it has its pitfalls. Even although this arrangement is agreed upon in advance, issues of jealously can and often arise. This kind of arrangement is strictly concerned with the couple's sexuality and does not reflect their day-to-day lifestyle as a couple.

Hotwifing is a grossly overused label to describe some relationship sexual dynamics. They often substitute it for cuckolding incorrectly. Like cuckolding, hotwifing removes the shared sexual partner experience of swinging and places the female (hotwife) as the sole recipient of adventure outside the marriage. The husband in this relationship is also aware and consents to her sexual exploits while he remains exclusive to her. Often, in a hotwife relationship, the husband will be a part of the sexual action beyond simply watching. This arrangement is usually initiated by the husband as he finds watching his wife being intimate with others to be mutually arousing. Like swinging, this arrangement often leads to feelings of jealousy and often is short-lived. Starting as a fantasy, it frequently disappears from the couple's repertoire within a short period of being lived out.

Cuckolding, ironically, is often the final landing point that many of the previous relationships end up. More often than not, there is a slow progression from swinging into hotwifing and then things either expire and the couple resumes a vanilla life or they move on to cuckolding. That being said, most successful cuckold couples bypass swinging altogether and often shift from hotwife to cuckoldress almost overnight.

I can not say this enough, cuckolding is not a sexual dynamic. It is a way of life that is organically driven from all corners of a person's existence. Sexually, emotionally, mentally, physically and even spiritually. The sex aspect is only a portion of the picture. To a cuckold, he has less than zero interest in having sex with other women. He is laser-focused on his wife and his wife only. Likewise, to a cuckoldress, the idea of seeing her husband with another woman, under any circumstances, is repugnant and can quickly destroy her on the inside. You can see why many swinging couples quickly move to cuckolding if the wife has any tendencies towards cuckoldry.

Two key fundamental elements separate cuckolding from hotwifing. With cuckolding, the husband has no sexual engagement during his wife's encounter with a bull (the other guy). They may allow him to please himself, if his cuckoldress permits, but his sexual satisfaction comes from her sexual satisfaction. The second element is all things outside the bedroom.

In this relationship, the cuckoldress maintains the alpha role (she wears the pants) almost at all times. The husband (cuckold) loses his identity to his wife. In simple terms, it means it directly correlates his pleasure to his wife's pleasure. It takes the cliche ' happy wife, happy life' literally. As previously mentioned, cuckolding substantially bends the power dynamics within the relationship. The husband is often degraded or humiliated. His fair share of household duties and financial contributions are as unfair as you can get. The cuckoldress becomes a Goddess for which he worships. There is no fairness. It is a one-sided, highly distorted way of running a relationship. And yet, it is extremely satisfying, enjoyable and rewarding to both partners.

How in the name of $%*$ is this possible? Simply put, their DNA. Deep within a cuckold and a cuckoldress, they have a psychology, a repressed need, a mindset that often they are unaware of. Cuckolding is the most effective, healthy and loving way that I'm aware of, that allows this need to finally come out and be actualized. The ultimate question is, do you have it?

Chapter Five
I DON'T KNOW IF I CAN DO THAT

I'm going to assume your husband has already done his research and has established he is, at heart, a cuckold. If you're reading this book ahead of him exploring his sexuality, I would encourage you both to read my companion book that examines his inclinations to cuckolding. You can find it here. Leaving the cuckold side of the equation for your husband to figure out, let's look at what makes a cuckoldress tick. I should warn you, I was born to be a cuckoldress and it may bias my opinions.

If you have come this far, there is a small piece of you that is curious. Perhaps even a tad excited? If so, do not feel guilty. You have done nothing wrong to want to understand how cuckolding works and why. If nothing else, you will have learned who you are not.

But...

Let's look at what being a cuckoldress is made of.

The obvious is a huge libido. If you have little to no sex drive, I encourage you to stop reading now. Don't waste your time. Your desire to please your husband by reading this book will end poorly. Simply tell him it's not for you and move on. You can't embrace being a cuckoldress if your sexuality is of little to no importance to you.

Going on the premise you have a healthy sex drive is a start. But not even close to enough. There is a door I want to open inside you but beware, it may trigger some negative self-talk. We all have a dark side. All I'm asking you to do is look inside and be brutally honest with yourself. You can lie to your husband, your friends, your parents and your children. Great. But to you, give yourself permission to think and explore without judgement.

Most women have been raised by their family and society to be good little girls. To be a selfless and loving daughter, wife and mother. To think of themselves last. To be proper and polite as much as possible. The idea of being promiscuous is shameful. Being submissive to your husband is your God-given duty.

Think I'm wrong? How does the word "slut" hit you? You think it to be a disgusting negative term used to describe a woman with no morals. How does the word "stud" hit you? A really hot looking guy that every girl wants to have a piece of, but can't have because he's too busy nailing as many other women as he can.

Sound about right? Seem fair that slut is bad. Very, very bad. Stud is good. Hot, even. THEY ARE THE SAME THING, except one refers to a woman and the other to a man. My point? They train you through your entire life to bury any desires that may be construed as being a bad girl. Who the hell made that rule up? That said, a large part of how you think and act is surface level. Let's go below that. Let's get to where you feel, in your secret world that you struggle to admit to yourself. This dark secret world of desire is why the book "50 Shades " was a blockbuster with so many women. It hit a vein that is very much there but deeply repressed.

If you have a large sexual appetite and desires that go beyond your husband, whom I'm sure you deeply love, then you are normal. Does that make you a cuckoldress? Nope. It could mean the other avenues (swinging or hotwifing) may be worth exploring. Having sex with someone who is essentially a stranger is scary. Few women can overcome the fear of this, even if everything else checks out. Then again, to live the life of a cuckoldress requires courage well above most, but there is one element about cuckolding that will appeal to some women only. They don't even fully recognize what it is. There is something about the dynamic that speaks to them beyond the sex. Beyond the power. Beyond the disparity. Those of you that are reading with eyes wide open know what it is but don't want to admit it. It's ugly. It's bad. It's wrong, just like the word slut?

Sadism. You need to enjoy inflicting emotional pain. In some deep way, you know it's wrong, but it feels so good. It caresses your soul so seductively. This is the complete opposite and complementary side of cuckolding that is a mandatory requirement for this kind of relationship. Your husband is an emotional masochist. He wants you to withhold sexual gratification from him and yet get yourself pleased by another man, usually while he suffers in frustration. He wants you to humiliate him and treat him like he is your little bitch. He loves when you spend his hard-earned money to buy sexy outfits to impress other men, not him. And you? You love doing all of it to him.

As I read my words, I think how harsh that must

sound to someone brand new to cuckolding. In reality, it is not harsh at all. It is an incredibly loving and freeing experience. Think about it. To know that your husband actually would prefer you to be a bad girl, that he wants to essentially be your slave. That's something that would horrify most men to admit, even if it were true. Like women, they are taught to be strong, demanding alphas in life.

You take that information and say "OMG, I love you BECAUSE you think this way" and then you add the "and I like being kinda cruel to you, manipulating you, controlling you...and you like me being that way?" It opens a door of freedom that is indescribable. It allows both of you to openly express the dark side that no one wants to admit, and yet the other person not only appreciates, but they also desire it.

It's a gigantic step to see, admit, and embrace this side. For many, having sadistic needs does not exist. If you are convinced that you fall in this camp, no matter how much you love your husband, you can never please him in a cuckolding relationship. How you deal with this is in the next chapter. For those of you that have an inkling I've struck a nerve, things are about to get very interesting for you and your hubby.

Chapter Six
WHAT IF I DON'T WANT TO

You have made it this far and for that, I'm sure your husband will be grateful. You have shown that you can be open-minded and that you care about his needs. You have likely read this book at his request. And now you need to tell him you're not interested (low libido) or it's just something you don't feel comfortable doing (you're missing the sadistic DNA). Both are acceptable reasons, and both should not be taken lightly.

Your husband needs to understand and respect your point of view. Together, you can figure other ways to satisfy his needs and yours. Perhaps the other alternative lifestyles discussed earlier may be an option for both of you. Maybe occasional roleplaying the cuckold marriage will be enough.

You need to understand your husband loves you more than anything. He does not want to hurt you or make you become someone you are not. But it's equally important for you to realize if he has come to you expressing a desire to look at cuckolding, he too can not be someone he is not. He may be an alpha male that is a take-control kinda guy in the boardroom and on the football field. But inside your marriage, he needs you to take control.

A girlfriend of mine once came to me asking for advice on this. She and her husband knew we had a cuckold marriage. Until that point, they were swingers. She did not feel like it was in her to be a cuckoldress in the true sense of the word and wanted to know how I would have handled it.

Instantly I told her to consider an FLR (Female Led Relationship) where she is in charge. It puts the husband in a submissive role within the marriage, but it stops there. It bypasses the humiliation, the sissification, the gentle emotional torture that a cuckoldress lives for.

If you are not into cuckolding, this is an extremely effective way to satisfy your cuckold husband, even although you refrain from being in the cuckoldress role. Alternatively, consider hotwifing, where you can enjoy the sexual components and also bypass the more comprehensive areas of cuckolding.

No matter what you do, do not lash out at your husband for making himself this vulnerable. It takes a tremendous amount of courage for a man to disclose this kind of thing to his wife. He will undoubtedly fear that you will think less of him or even worse, want to leave him after he has admitted he wants to be a metaphorical wimp. Also, recognize he has disclosed this to you because he can no longer keep his desires inside. You can't just say "nope" and forget it ever happened.

Davie and I have lived this way for over 7 years and, have met a lot of couples that also honor cuckolding in the marriage. All of us have agreed, just like coming out of the closet for being gay, you CAN NOT go back into the closet. Once your husband reaches a point where he feels compelled to tell you he is a cuckold, you can't undo that. Whether or not you like it, your husband is and always will be a cuckold. The ideal situation is you know this kind of information BEFORE you get married but often, it's so deeply repressed (yes, even with men) that they only discover this side of themselves later on.

Consider his cuck DNA to be a humongous gift. Many women would kill to be with a man that is this open. A man that puts his wife so high up on a pedestal with so much freedom and nothing but admiration and yes, even for her dark side. Be grateful. Be gentle and be true to yourself. Tell him it's not for you but be willing to find ways as a couple to navigate a way where both of you come out satisfied and feeling good about yourselves.

Chapter Seven
SO WHAT IF I TELL HIM I'M EXCITED?

*G*irl, be aware. If you have been asked to read this book by your husband and he is waiting for your feedback, you have only one chance to see how he feels for real. Refer him to this chapter if things go wrong. What I'm about to suggest is simply validation for you to see how he really feels about cuckolding. I don't recommend doing this 'just to see' but, rather, to confirm to yourself that he is solid in his resolve to be cuckolded.

Make sure you are alone with him in an undisturbed environment. Sit down, smile, and look him directly in the eyes. Then, as uncomfortable as it may feel, ask him to drop his pants. Yes, he will look at you wondering if you're about to please him or what. DO NOT MOVE. Now tell him to stand in the middle of the room with his bottom half completely exposed. He'll look at you like you have 2 heads. Again, smile and tell him to just do it. Ideally, do this at a random time when talking about your relationship, sex or cuckolding has not been on the table.

Once he has his pants on the ground, smile and say you

have been reading this book. It has made you think a lot about who you are and who he is. Then tell him you feel kind of scared to say what you want to say because you're afraid he will get upset. Trust me when I say he will NOT get upset. He will either look at you with pleading puppy dog eyes or he will verbally assure you he will not get upset and for you to continue.

Pause. Smile. Take a deep breath and then tell him you really like the idea of being able to fuck other guys if he is okay with it. Don't look away from his eyes. Continue by telling him that the more you think about it, the more you feel you kind of deserve it given his small dick. Stop talking, point to his cock, and watch it grow faster than the speed of light.

Case closed. A man can lie till he is blue in the face. His cock can not! If he is hard, which if you keep talking like that, it will be rock hard, you dear, have a little cucky as a husband. Congratulations!

If he is not hard, have him read this section of the book. All you are trying to do is firmly establish if cuckolding is a real thing with him. If it is not, you both need to discuss issues that are beyond this book.

Going forward, I will assume he has proven his DNA in an outward physical way. This is the ideal time to talk beyond the b.s. You both have some deep and dark inner desires that you have likely hid from everyone (including yourselves). Rejoice in knowing you can finally open up. To get in touch with that inner devil that has been trampled down for so many years.

I remember when davie and I had The Conversation. By the end, we were both sitting on the couch playing with ourselves in uncontrollable excitement. The look of sheer joy on his face was priceless. I can honestly say, I don't think I had seen him that hard ever. As we talked, I got so wet I had to change my panties.

Enjoy the freedom you are feeling. Be gentle, but also be brave. You have opened Pandora's box. The natural reaction when such a huge revelation is made by two people is to want to dump stuff. It's like you have finally found someone you can talk to about it. Don't worry about what's next at this point. Just enjoy the banter and wait for a few days before you sit down together to explore things with a little more thought.

I can not stress enough, DO NOT DO THIS, if being a cuckoldress is not calling you loud and clear. Just as this little test will help you find out his legitimacy, it should also validate your feelings. Telling the man you love that you would like to fuck other guys is just plain mean. BUT, if you have that sadistic side, it will kind of turn you on. You may be nervous or scared, but also a little excited. In going through this very simple exercise, your heart will ultimately give you answers that may seem wrong but feel oh, so good.

Chapter Eight
ESTABLISHING BOUNDRIES

Once you have both revealed that cuckolding is a direction you would like to explore as a couple, you need to give yourselves some time to let things settle and digest. You will probably think of situations you feel uncomfortable about or situations you want to avoid. You may even have second thoughts about the whole thing. Normal. Natural. You need that breathing space to let these kinds of issues bubble up before you sit down and discuss moving forward with any seriousness.

I have a companion book "Advanced Couples Guide Edition" that will help take your newly established cuckold marriage to a new level. I would not recommend you as an "advanced couple" for at least a year. You want to let things unfold in baby steps. Explore the power shift, both in and out of the bedroom.

Ultimately, you will reach a point where it will be time to cross the final threshold to solidify your cuckoldress status-having sex with another man. Believe me, exciting times are ahead. In the meantime, this is a huge barrier to cross. Perhaps the most critical part of having a healthy, loving and loyal cuckold marriage is based on these very tender initial stages of crossing the final line.

I know I keep saying this but please, please, please, take your time as a couple. Do not be in a hurry to go out and fuck other guys. Roleplay. Absolutely. In fact, I'd insist on hard role-playing before you get to the real deal. You need to know your boundaries. You need to feel natural being sadistic. It is within you. You have just repressed this side of who you are for so long, it will take time to catch up to your new reality. Remember, in this kind of relationship, your sadism is the single kindest, most loving thing you can do for your husband. He not only loves it, he truly craves it. It makes him feel whole and complete.

All that being said, both of you will have your limits. You may have a hard time telling him to leave his cage on because he needs to be trained properly. You may feel extremely uncomfortable with him being present when you finally get intimate with another guy. He may not have any interest in serving your bull in any way. Perhaps he also does not want to be in the same room when you do the deed, or maybe he feels it to be necessary. These issues all need discussion BEFORE anything happens.

It is impossible to cover every scenario that may cause either of you emotional discomfort, but try to be as exhaustive as possible. Neither of you should move forward until you agree on all contentious areas. It's also worth noting that the beginning stages of what you're both cool with will change.

As he learns to become more compliant and internalizes his place, he will accept and fully embrace his role as your cuckyboy. He will begin to feel significantly more at ease to submit to you on almost all requests you have. Likewise, as you travel the path of self-indulgence and self-confidence, understanding your sadistic side becomes a win-win for both of you. You will also find yourself feeling more comfortable in areas I'm reserving for my advanced couples guide.

If you try to speed up your progression into cuckoldry as a couple, it is almost a guarantee for big troubles. If you are one of those couples that have already embarked on other alternative lifestyle paths (swinging/hotwifing/BDSM), you may move a little quicker, but remember, cuckolding is a unique kind of marriage. It pushes the limits on people's dark side. It takes all that is considered bad and ugly by society and puts it on a pedestal. This converse logic is largely why it makes it so special and addictive. You both get a taste of a life that is just not allowed but is very much legal (assuming it is a consenting arrangement).

My loose guideline is 3-2-1. You both should take 3 months (min.) just to self examine and think if cuckolding is for you personally. You should then take at least 2 months (min.) to discuss it between each other. Do nothing except talk and begin exploring the dynamic within the confines of your bedroom. Finally, you need a month to play the idea out in test runs. Then and only then should you even think about setting up a situation that will allow you to cross the line.

What do I mean by "test runs"?

This is where you both acknowledge that proceeding further is a good thing. You want to see if there are any cracks in the cuckold foundation. Let's face it. You're about to inflict the ultimate degree of emotional pain on your husband, which you love dearly. He is about to feel things he has no idea how to manage (cuckold angst). He'll agree to essentially use a few good men that you have no intention of going all the way. Yes, it seems kind of cruel but believe me, they will not care. You'll give them many months of spank bank materiel. You are doing what I like to call INTENTIONAL FALSE STARTS.

Chapter Nine
INTENTIONAL FALSE STARTS

Though INTENTIONAL FALSE STARTS is a rather simple concept, I felt it's importance warranted a section unto itself. If you are a couple already into swinging or hotwifing, I recommend skipping this section. The sacredness of monogamy is something you have already gone way beyond.

A false start is exactly what you think it is. You start with the outward illusion of going all the way, but pull back and end BEFORE things cross set boundaries. Perhaps your husband has no emotional reservations about seeing you go down on another guy but is adamantly opposed to seeing you kiss him. Perhaps it's the other way around.

Maybe you feel that vaginal penetration is the only line that will make you feel you have crossed the line of monogamy. Each person's line will be different. Establish your limits as a couple and agree to the farthest you can go without compromising either of you, so you don't feel you have now crossed the line.

Then hook up with another man. No, he does not have to be a bull in this case. He can be some random guy you both see at a bar or social club or sex club. Begin flirting, caressing, touching, fondling, kissing, licking or whatever is the last stop before it crosses lines. Stay at this metaphorical line for as long as you can. DO NOT CROSS THE LINE, but edge as close as possible.

You are doing this to simulate the ultimate experience without the damage. It will allow both your husband (soon to be cuckold) and yourself an opportunity to feel all the excitement and potential damage while retaining an escape route if needed. For those of you that are convinced it needs no such foreplay, have at her, but beware that once that last line is crossed, you can never go back.

Cuckolding is deeply rooted in sexuality, absolutely. But it is much more about taking your relationship in all areas to a whole new level. Fuck it up and it will all be in vain. It should be driven primarily out of love for each other, not sex. This is a key point that the porn world ignores altogether. There is so much focus on the sex. Sex sex sex. Yes, the sex is nuclear. It's also about the power and freedom denied or given. But as I have repeatedly said, it is about two people who love each other deeply. They reach such a level of openness and comfort that they disclose their deepest, darkest and ugliest desires that their partner not only accepts, but also turns them on. Therein is the true magic, the true essence of cuckolding.

Giving yourselves a couple of intentional false starts helps secure the integrity of your relationship will remain intact, regardless. Yes, it's kind of mean for the "other guy" but cuckolding is not about the other guy. It's about the two of you, your marriage sex life and being given the gift to become who you really are with your partner's support.

Chapter Ten
LOOK OUT FOR THE ANGST

Cuckold angst. I get a little upset at this term. It focuses on the cuckold and all his fears, anxieties and esteem issues being temporarily damaged because of your playtime with a bull. What about the cuckoldress's feelings of guilt, shame and regret? Does she not experience a similar backslide of emotions?

I prefer to call it "angst", period, full stop. It is felt in different ways and at different times by both the man and the woman, but they both have waves of emotions that are primarily exclusive to this kind of relationship.

Even although the cuck is not only aware of but also encourages his wife to sleep with other guys, she is still likely to feel guilt and shame. Similarly, the cuck knows his wife loves him; she has likely provided multiple roadblocks and showed she only wants him sexually, and yet he will feel tidal waves of jealousy and self-loathing. He is absurdly turned on and bitterly hates that it turns him on.

In both cases, the common ground is it can be intense

emotions that can occur before, during, or after an encounter with a bull. If we mismanage it, it can prove disastrous. You both need to be very much aware that you will have these feelings before they occur. Just knowing that in advance will help both of you help yourselves and each other. Know that these feelings are ALWAYS only temporary and are rooted in unfounded life values that have been driven into both of you from a very young age. As you move forward and learn to manage these feelings, they happen less often and with rapidly decreasing intensity.

Before you cross that final line that I discussed in the previous section, make sure you talk this out. Intentional false starts are designed to let both of you start to feel this without it becoming too damaging. Additionally, it gives you both a chance to talk about it afterward privately, so you are much better equipped to handle the emotional roller coaster you are about to get on once the real deal begins.

This should not intimidate you, but rather excite you. My davie was frankly a mess on my first encounter with a bull. Neither of us was prepared. He fell apart when we got home and began bawling his eyes out. That reaction sent me straight into a sewer of negative self talk about how horrible a person I must have been and how unforgivably ashamed of myself I became. Fast forward almost eight years, we both look back at that night and laugh. It's still one of the more exciting times we had because it was soooo intense.

Over time, you will learn to help your cuckold deal with his angst whenever it shows up. You'll also recognize when angst is creeping into his mind BEFORE he is aware of it. Likewise, he will learn to support and encourage you so you know you are doing nothing wrong and should feel good about yourself. You deserve this life and you are making him happier than he ever thought possible. It becomes a real win-win situation.

Chapter Eleven
BUYERS REGRET - OH THE GUILT

Buyers regret sucks. The aftermath of buying that new fitness device or food processing tool that collects dust seven minutes after we have opened the package. It's the feeling you get when you reflect and say "I shouldn't have done that". With cuckolding, this manifests into angst.

With the products you regret buying, you can usually just return them or exchange them for something else. With your husband/wife, it doesn't work that simple. The only way out of it is to accept it and start developing strategies to minimize feeling it.

I don't want to mislead anyone here, eliminating angst is just not possible. In fact, for the cuckold, it slowly forms an essential part of who they are and what they need to feel whole. For the cuckoldress, she learns to process these feelings and over time, learns to pivot her angst to throw it back at her cuck to accentuate the entire experience for both.

I encourage you and particularly your cuck to read

my DNA Of A Cuckold book (husband edition) where I go into significant details on helping him understand what you are likely going through emotionally and how he can help. Coles notes version is it must remain rock solid during an encounter with a bull. He needs to continually praise you and reassure you that your actions are deeply appreciated. He needs to understand you are now the driver of the relationship. If you are not in the mood to be with a bull, he must respect that no matter how much he craves seeing you scream for more from your bull.

How can you possibly help your cuckold husband through his emotional meltdowns? Think about cuckolding as a relationship dynamic. The entire thing is completely upside down from normal social standards. There is no equality. There is little reciprocity, and the female wears the pants. The same upside-down logic is the ideal way you need to develop to help your loving cuck work through his turbulence.

You see him crying or becoming outwardly aggressive with anger, logic would suggest you comfort him with love and gentleness or you become apologetic for your actions of playing with a bull. WRONG WRONG WRONG.

What's the opposite (upside down)way to this? No sympathy. No comfort. No soft sensitivity. He is driven by your ferocious sex god status. Own it. Everything you are doing in part to please him. Moreover, you are doing it in part because you need to be in charge, selfish, self-indulgent, cruel. All words that primarily have negative associations with them. But with your cuck, they are all good things. Things he loves about you. Things he craves about you. You have finally permitted yourself to let your inner beast out. You like it, and now your cuck will unintentionally steal from you?

No way! You deserve to be a cuckoldress. You should feel no shame, no guilt and no regret. Your cuck needs to understand that this was and always has been an inevitable outcome of your marriage. You were meant to be. It is a beautiful, kind and loving gift you have both given each other. Be happy for yourself. Rejoice to know that he is feeling the angst. He needs to feel it. Please trust me when I tell you, once he is past that moment, he will thank you and be grateful.

Frankly, the best thing you can do to help him get through his little cry baby moments is to tell him to suck it up. It's who you both are. He needs to stop fighting it and start rejoicing in it. I know it seems counter-intuitive, but it is the best thing you can do.

When you sense he is about to enter his little pity party, whether it's as your getting ready to meet a bull, in the act of or after the fact...ALWAYS know, you are his goddess. You have total control over his action and his emotions. With that much control comes a ton of responsibility. Don't take this light-heartedly. Handle it the way you think you should and it will make things worse. Be firm, be loving, but most importantly, be honest. He is now your cuckold. You own his soul. He needs to suck it up or you will need to stake your claim in some real, tangible ways.

Chapter Twelve

STAKING YOUR CLAIM

*I*nevitably, your relationship will slowly shift from a traditional monogamous marriage into a cuckold marriage. Contrary to all porn, this does not happen overnight or after the first time you "cuck" (have sex with a bull) your husband. As I continue to drive home, cuckolding is way more than sex. It is an all-encompassing shift in power dynamics. It's a mutual agreement between two people who deeply love each other and want the best for the other person.

That "best" is not only permitting them but also encouraging them to fully immerse themselves in their deep-seated but fully repressed dark side. The sadistic/masochistic part of their brain that functions almost like emotional cocaine when activated.

Once you have both experienced living in the sex lifestyle of cuckolding for a while, there should be a growing comfort you have with each other to open things up even more. I'm specifically referring to areas of your relationship that exist when Mr. Bull is MIA.

Repeatedly, you have shown your sexual appetite to your cuck as exceeding anything he could hope to achieve. That story has been told and done. You have both experienced the sadomasochistic side of your sexuality. He has been deprived and you have probably started having some of the best sex of your life. But what about that innate need you both have when it's not wet and wild?

He craves to feel some degree of emotional pain. It could be as humiliation, degradation or just feeling like he is your little princess. It makes him, in his own loving way, feel better inside. It just feels right. It feels good.

You crave that feeling of ultimate control, power and unconditional freedom to have your world revolve around you. It feels like a dream that would never really come true.

Guess what? This dream is now your reality. Beyond the financial constraints of what you and your cuckold husband have, you can have ANYTHING you want. This is the premise of my fourth book installment to this series (Advanced Couples Edition) which I will only briefly touch on here.

Once you have staked your claim as being his cuckold Goddess in the bedroom, you need to finish the evolution of the cuckold dynamic to complete and fully actualize all the rewards this marriage offers. This is where the lines of an FLR (Female Led Relationship) and a Cuckold Marriage become blurry.

Leaving the disparity, humiliation and control in the bedroom will soon become unsatisfying for both of you. After several encounters with a bull, this will leak into other areas of your marriage. This is a wonderful thing. Don't be reluctant to maintain your Goddess status once the dust settles. Your cuckold is yours. He is for you and you alone. You are his Goddess. You essentially own his soul. Be careful to manage him, but always put your love for each other as paramount as you grow.

If you want to relax after a hard day of work and have a delicate glass of wine while you chat to a bull, do so. Cucky husband would love to help you achieve that goal and will be eager to help make the dinner while you chat. Perhaps you want to go shopping to pick out a sexy outfit for your next bull. Perfect. It will give cucky time to finish doing your laundry, for which he will probably have a hard-on the entire time.

It is a hard thing to get your head around, but once you have repeatedly crossed the cuckold lines sexually, it will empower you mentally and emotionally to carry it forward. To the outside world, it seems ruthless, unfair and showing no love for your husband. You will have realized it is a very loving, deeply appreciated and kind thing that you are allowing your cuck to do. It will make both of you happy and can strengthen an emotional bond that is already rock solid.

It does not get better. After seven years, I'm not sure I even remember how to cook or clean anymore. Lol.

Chapter Thirteen
MANAGEMENT AND LONG TERM - THE NEW YOU

Where do you go from here? Can this fairytale last without one of us snapping? Yes, it can last. As I mentioned at the onset of this book, many studies have shown cuckold marriages are the most extreme in both ways. They either fall apart very quickly or they are one of the most satisfying, successful relationships out there. It is very little in between. It works, or it doesn't.

I also want to remind you, cuckolding IS NOT for everyone. For most, it will not work. Despite what many other "experts" in the field may tell you, cuckolding is not something everyone should try or, that it will work if you just learn to communicate or even worse, that you can convert your husband or wife into being in this kind of relationship. NO NO NO! It works at such a deep and profound level because it is the culmination of two very special types of people. There are no other options. Anything else will cause ultimate destruction, eventually.

This is precisely why I have put together this series of non-fiction books to help couples navigate their way into or out of this life. For davie and I, we were born to be in a cuckold marriage. It is beautiful and it just works perfectly. Unfortunately, we have seen many couples come and go, many ending in a dissolved marriage. Why? The short answer. They made a bunch of assumptions about what it takes, who you need to be, and how it works.

With that, just like with any relationship (yes, even friends), you will have your bumps along the way. For cuckold couples, those bumps are huge and many in the first 1-2 years. Once you get past deprogramming yourselves and each other from societal norms and accept that being the way you are is awesome for the other person, things click.

However, we still have our occasional spats. Some little insecurities or moments of not thinking things through. It would be impossible for me to itemize each point of contention davie and I have. Usually, they are issues surrounding our kids and how we should raise them. Some issues come up about our sex play, but that is usually a problem of us both wanting more of the same thing, which is later laughed about.

Where things need focus is maintaining an ongoing, non-stop open communication about EVERYTHING. Most arguing occurs because there is a misunderstanding or you have failed to see the other person's point of view. Talking eradicates this in a hurry.

As you both travel the path of cuckoldry, you will both change as people. To the outside world, they will notice little, but to each other, there will be enormous changes over time. Given your innate dispositions, this is a wonderful thing. You will become more and more comfortable being selfish and not feeling guilty. You begin to get turned on just by calling your cuck a little girl at the grocery store where others will overhear. Simultaneously, your cuck will mutually look forward to sitting in the back seat while you drive the girls to soccer practise sitting upfront. He will begin to submit to all your requests without challenge, making your daily life more harmonious than you thought ever possible.

As long as you keep talking through the entire journey, you will find the need to pinch yourself to confirm it's not a dream. However, I should also caution you, this trajectory is likely only to last for a while. Given both of your primal needs for inflicting or receiving emotional pain, you will eventually need more than what I call the vanilla cuck. This is when you will want to up the ante even more.

Be very careful when you hit this ceiling. Outside of starting a cuckold marriage, this is the next phase that can prove itself messy if not managed, planned and executed with the primary goal of mutual love in the forefront.

I have left this level of cuckolding intentionally out of this book to avoid scaring some people away from a life that they were born to live. Moving to the more extreme degrees of cuckolding is not for all cuck couples. Many are happy to remain where we left here. For those of you that want to explore deeper levels of intrinsic satisfaction (sissification, cuck clean ups, cuck cages and forced Chasity and financial domination (find)) I would encourage you to consider picking up my 4th volume in this series that deals with offering ideas to explore as a couple, managing the issues as you go deeper and hard maintenance or escape hatches from the lifestyle.

From the bottom of our hearts, thank you so much for your time and both davie and I wish you and your little hubby the very best, no matter which way you go.

Hugs,
A xo

PRAISE FOR ALLORA SINCLAIR

"Speechless. I am without speech. This is incredible stuff."
Dana

"What a wonderful contribution. I'm not sure if I should thank my hubby or Allora more."
Nicole

"This made telling my wife so much easier. I didn't know where to start. Allora takes the conversation from the beginning and explains everything in such a thorough and sensitive way."
William and Bonnie

"Nick and I are so grateful. Allora has helped us redirect into a world we both wanted but were afraid to tell each other about. Her books made the whole journey so much more easy."
Karen and Nick

"When I told my husband I couldn't do this kind of thing, Allora helped me realize that I'm very lucky to be given this opportunity even if it's not for me. You never know, I may still change my mind."

    Sara

ALSO BY ALLORA SINCLAIR

DNA OF A CUCKOLD - THE MISSING LINK

DNA OF A CUCKOLD - HUSBAND EDITION

DNA OF A CUCKOLD - ADVANCED COUPLES

THE MENTOR - 15 YEARS EARLIER- Prologue

THE MENTOR 1 - A BAD INFLUENCE

THE MENTOR 2 - THE INFLUENCE GETS STRONGER

THE MENTOR 3 - COMPLETE INFLUENCE

CUCKOLD ADDICTION - FIGHT IT OR EMBRACE IT?

BAD GIRLS - THE GUIDE TO FEMALE POWER

ABOUT THE AUTHOR

Allora Sinclair is a happily married 40 year old. She and her loving cuckold husband Dave (davie) have been in a cuckold marriage for over seven years and she has now decided to start documenting their journey from vanilla to a complete FLR relationship. If Allora is not found at her computer or out shopping for shoes, she is usually found in the caring arms of davie or embraced in ecstasy with one of her favourite bulls. She has done a series of non-fiction books to help couples navigate their way through the heavily distorted life of being a cuckold couple. She is now working on a series of fiction books that are based on some of their real-life experiences. If you like what she's doing, please leave a review wherever you purchased this book.

Made in United States
Troutdale, OR
04/22/2024